Lerner SPORTS™

GREATEST OF ALL TIME PLAYERS

G.O.A.T. FOOTBALL CORNERBACKS

Audrey Stewart

Lerner Publications ◆ Minneapolis

Lerner Publications Company
An imprint of Lerner Publishing Group, Inc.
241 First Avenue North
Minneapolis, MN 55401 USA

For reading levels and more information, look up this title at www.lernerbooks.com.

Main body text set in Aptifer Sans LT Pro.
Typeface provided by Linotype AG.

Library of Congress Cataloging-in-Publication Data

Names: Stewart, Audrey, author.
Title: G.O.A.T. football cornerbacks / Audrey Stewart.
Other titles: Greatest of all time football cornerbacks
Description: Minneapolis, MN : Lerner Publications, [2025] | Series: Greatest of all time players | Includes bibliographical references and index. | Audience: Ages 7–11 | Audience: Grades 2–3 | Summary: "Cornerbacks are often the fastest and most-talented players on a football team's defense. The best cornerbacks can shut down opposing wide receivers. Meet the greatest cornerbacks in NFL history and rank them for yourself"—Provided by publisher.
Identifiers: LCCN 2023048811 (print) | LCCN 2023048812 (ebook) | ISBN 9798765625811 (library binding) | ISBN 9798765628775 (paperback) | ISBN 9798765633762 (epub)
Subjects: LCSH: Cornerbacks (Football)—United States—Biography—Juvenile literature. | Football players—United States—Biography—Juvenile literature.
Classification: LCC GV939.A1 S73 2025 (print) | LCC GV939.A1 (ebook) | DDC 796.332092/2—dc23/eng/20231027

LC record available at https://lccn.loc.gov/2023048811
LC ebook record available at https://lccn.loc.gov/2023048812

Manufactured in the United States of America
1 – CG – 7/15/24

TABLE OF CONTENTS

Seattle Seahawks cornerback Richard Sherman (*right*) reaches to block a pass during the 2014 National Football Conference championship game.

CATCH AND RUN!

The Seattle Seahawks played the San Francisco 49ers in the National Football Conference (NFC) championship game in January 2014. At the start of the fourth quarter, the Seahawks were losing 17–13. Seahawks quarterback Russell Wilson quickly threw a touchdown pass to give Seattle the lead. With 30 seconds left to play, the Seahawks led 23–17, but the 49ers were moving down the field.

FACTS AT A GLANCE

- CORNERBACK **ROD WOODSON** HOLDS THE NATIONAL FOOTBALL LEAGUE (NFL) RECORD FOR INTERCEPTIONS RETURNED FOR TOUCHDOWNS WITH 12.
- **DEION SANDERS** WAS BOTH A PRO BASEBALL PLAYER AND A SUPERSTAR CORNERBACK IN THE NFL.
- EVEN THOUGH **KEN RILEY** WAS A TOP PLAYER THROUGHOUT HIS CAREER, HE WASN'T A FIRST-TEAM ALL-PRO UNTIL HIS FINAL NFL SEASON.
- **CHAMP BAILEY** IS THE YOUNGEST PLAYER IN NFL HISTORY TO RECORD THREE INTERCEPTIONS IN A GAME.

The 49ers were on an eight-game winning streak and were not ready to break it. But they weren't prepared for Seahawks cornerback Richard Sherman. Sherman was up against 49ers receiver Michael Crabtree. Crabtree ran to receive a pass, but Sherman swatted the ball away. Sherman tipped the ball into a teammate's hands who caught the ball for an

interception. Sherman's great play helped the Seahawks win and earn their second trip to the Super Bowl.

The first role of a cornerback is to cover the other team's wide receivers. Their second job is to defend against running plays. Cornerbacks try to get the ball from the opposite team by forcing a fumble or an interception.

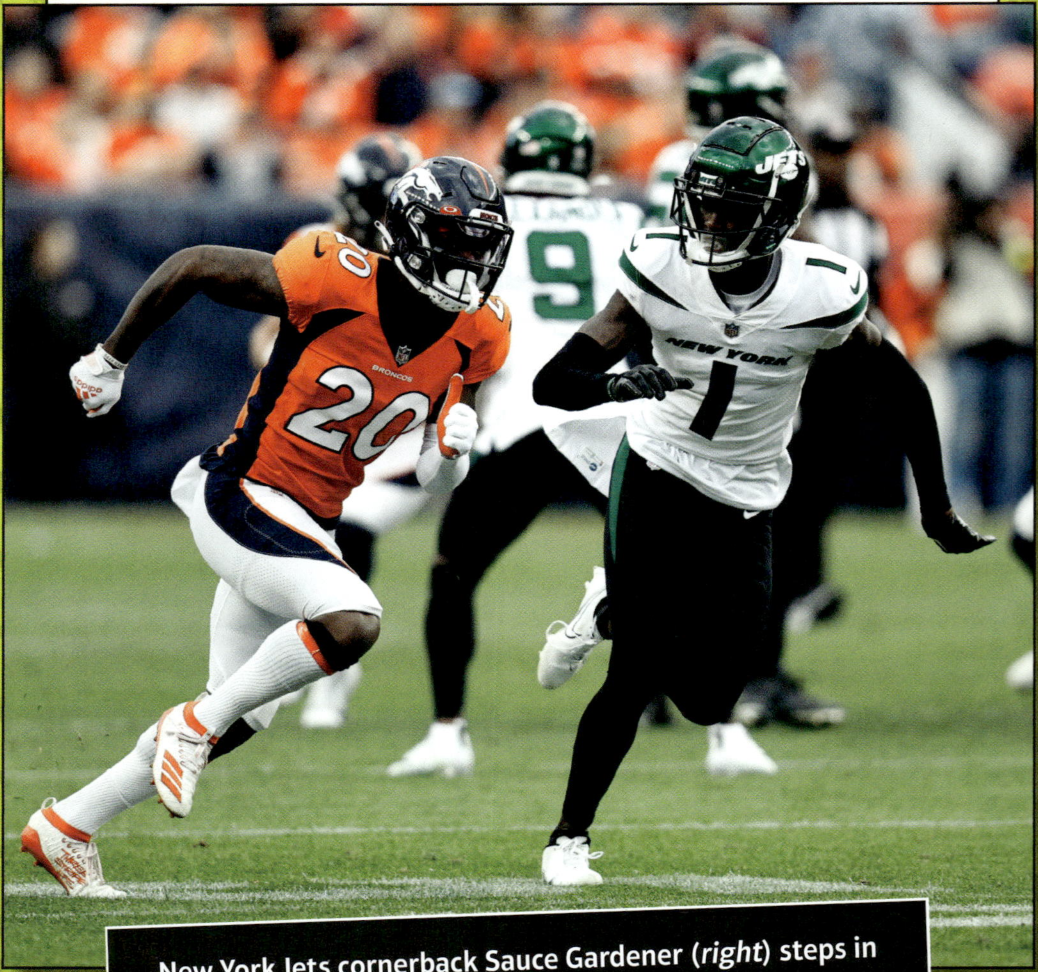

New York Jets cornerback Sauce Gardener (*right*) steps in front of a Denver Broncos wide receiver to slow him down.

Cornerback Stephon Gilmore of the New England Patriots won the NFL Defensive Player of the Year award in 2019.

Cornerbacks must be amazing athletes and fast thinkers. They run backward, turn fast, and sprint to catch their opponents to prevent them from scoring a touchdown. Cornerbacks know when and where to look for the ball. And cornerbacks aren't afraid to tackle another player, making cornerbacks a key part of a team's defense. Since 1971, six cornerbacks have won the NFL Defensive Player of the Year award.

NO. 10 RICHARD SHERMAN

Richard Sherman joined the Seattle Seahawks in 2011. Two years later, he led the NFL in interceptions with eight. He also finished the regular season with two recovered fumbles and 48 tackles.

Sherman helped the Seahawks win the 2014 Super Bowl as part of the team's Legion of Boom defense. He spent seven total seasons with the Seahawks. He played in four Pro Bowls and was a First-Team All-Pro in 2012, 2013, and 2014.

In 2018, Sherman started playing for the San Francisco 49ers. He had four interceptions and 116 tackles in three seasons with the team. He also played in one Pro Bowl and was part of the NFL 2010s All-Decade Team. His fellow football players ranked him 28th on the NFL Top 100 Players of 2020 list. Sherman finished his career with 37 interceptions and 495 tackles. After he retired from playing, he became a TV sports announcer.

RICHARD SHERMAN STATS

Fumbles Recovered	7
Touchdowns	4
Interceptions	37
Longest Interception Return	58 Yards

NO. 9 CHAMP BAILEY

Champ Bailey was a rare cornerback who was great at making big tackles and knocking down passes. He started his career with the Washington Redskins in 1999. He moved to the Denver Broncos in 2004 and intercepted a pass in his first game with the team.

Bailey could leap high into the air for interceptions. One standout game was during the playoffs against the New

England Patriots in 2006. Patriots quarterback Tom Brady threw a pass to an open receiver. But Bailey leaped and intercepted the ball. He ran it back 100 yards, just short of the end zone. It was Bailey's longest playoff interception return, and the Broncos won the game 27–13. Bailey led the NFL in interceptions for the 2006 season.

In his final NFL season, Bailey played in his first Super Bowl. He recorded four tackles, but the Broncos lost to the Seattle Seahawks. Bailey played in the Pro Bowl 12 times, the most ever for a cornerback. He retired in 2014 and became part of the Pro Football Hall of Fame in 2019.

CHAMP BAILEY STATS

Fumbles Recovered	6
Touchdowns	5
Interceptions	52
Longest Interception Return	70 Yards

NO. 8 MIKE HAYNES

The New England Patriots picked Mike Haynes in the first round of the 1976 NFL Draft. Haynes played seven seasons with the Patriots. He started 86 games and recorded 28 interceptions during that time.

In 1983, Haynes joined the Los Angeles Raiders. That season, Haynes helped the Raiders beat the Washington

Redskins in the 1984 Super Bowl 38–9. In 1984, Haynes made a 97-yard interception return in a game against the Miami Dolphins, which was a team record at that time. His partner on the team was fellow cornerback Lester Hayes. They were one of the best cornerback pairs in NFL history.

Haynes was a fast and smart player. He could stay close to any player he was guarding. He stopped some of the league's best wide receivers during his 14-year NFL career. Haynes was a First-Team All-Pro player in 1984 and 1985. He played in the Pro Bowl nine times.

MIKE HAYNES STATS

Fumbles Recovered	12
Touchdowns	5
Interceptions	46
Longest Interception Return	97 Yards

NO. 7 DARRELL GREEN

Darrell Green was the last pick in the first round of the 1983 NFL Draft. But Green turned out to be one of the best Washington Redskins players for 20 seasons. Green finished his first season fourth on the team for tackles with 109.

During the 1987 season, Green recorded a career-high three interceptions in a game against the Detroit Lions. Green and Washington advanced to the Super Bowl that season and won

42–10 against the Denver Broncos. Washington claimed another Super Bowl win in 1992 against the Buffalo Bills.

Green had a long career. His longest interception returned for a touchdown was in 1997, his 15th season. Green ran 83 yards for a touchdown against the Philadelphia Eagles. He is the oldest player with an interception return for a touchdown and an interception return of at least 80 yards. He played his final season with Washington in 2002.

DARRELL GREEN STATS

Fumbles Recovered	10
Touchdowns	8
Interceptions	54
Longest Interception Return	83 Yards

NO. 6

KEN RILEY

Ken Riley's pro football career started in 1969. He played his entire 15-season career with the Cincinnati Bengals. Although he was one of the league's top players, he was not a First-Team All-Pro until his final season.

In his first five seasons in the NFL, Riley recorded 18 interceptions. In 1976, he had a career-high nine interceptions. His best game that season was against the New York Jets.

Riley recorded three interceptions, and the Bengals beat the Jets 42–3.

Riley recorded 65 career interceptions, a Bengals record. He holds several other Bengals records, including five interceptions returned for touchdowns and 596 total interception return yards. Only Ron Woodson has recorded more interceptions since Riley retired in 1983. Riley was the head football coach at Florida A&M University from 1986 to 1993. He joined the Pro Football Hall of Fame in 2023.

KEN RILEY STATS

Fumbles Recovered	18
Touchdowns	5
Interceptions	65
Longest Interception Return	66 Yards

NO. 5 RONNIE LOTT

The San Francisco 49ers picked Ronnie Lott eighth overall in the 1981 NFL Draft. Lott began his NFL career with seven interceptions in his first season. His outstanding rookie performance helped the 49ers win the 1982 Super Bowl. Lott won three more Super Bowls with the 49ers in 1985,

1989, and 1990. He is one of only five 49ers players to be part of all four of the team's Super Bowl wins.

Lott was great at hitting, tackling, and jumping over his opponents to grab the ball. His passion and leadership on the field were recognized by his teammates year after year. Lott was a First-Team All-Pro six times and played in the Pro Bowl 10 times. He led the NFL in interceptions twice. Lott is a member of the College Football Hall of Fame, the Pro Football Hall of Fame, and the International Sports Hall of Fame.

RONNIE LOTT STATS

Fumbles Recovered	17
Touchdowns	5
Interceptions	63
Longest Interception Return	83 Yards

NO. 4 RICHARD LANE

In 1952, Richard Lane showed some newspaper clippings about his college and US Army football games to the Los Angeles Rams and asked for a tryout. The Rams hired Lane, and he had an outstanding rookie season. Known for his speed and strength, "Night Train" Lane broke the NFL record for interceptions with 14. The following season, he blocked a field goal against the Green Bay Packers and ran the ball back 45 yards for a touchdown.

From 1954 through 1959, Lane played for the Chicago Cardinals. He led the NFL in interceptions and interception return yards in 1954. In his six seasons with the Cardinals, Lane logged 30 interceptions and played in four Pro Bowls. In 1960, as part of the Detroit Lions, Lane returned an interception for an 80-yard touchdown. The great play helped Detroit win their first game of the season. A knee injury forced Lane to retire in 1965.

RICHARD LANE STATS

Fumbles Recovered	11
Touchdowns	8
Interceptions	68
Longest Interception Return	80 Yards

NO. 3 DEION SANDERS

In 1989, Deion Sanders joined the Atlanta Falcons as a cornerback and the New York Yankees as an outfielder. He played Major League Baseball for nine seasons and NFL football for 14 seasons. Nicknamed Prime Time, Sanders intercepted 24 passes during his five seasons with the Falcons. In 1993, Sanders recorded seven interceptions.

Sanders joined the San Francisco 49ers in 1994. This was

the best season of his career. He caught six interceptions and returned three for touchdowns. Two of his touchdown returns were for 90 or more yards. He was the first player in NFL history to do this. Sanders is a two-time Super Bowl champion. He won in 1995 with the 49ers and in 1996 with the Dallas Cowboys. He has also played in eight Pro Bowls. Sanders is tied for fifth all-time for interceptions returned for touchdowns with nine. He became a college football coach in 2020.

DEION SANDERS STATS

Fumbles Recovered	13
Touchdowns	22
Interceptions	53
Longest Interception Return	93 Yards

NO. 2 CHARLES WOODSON

Charles Woodson played 18 NFL seasons. He started his career in 1988 with the Oakland Raiders. Woodson played in the Pro Bowl in each of his first four seasons. After eight seasons with the Raiders, he joined the Green Bay Packers.

With the Packers, Woodson proved again that he was one of the best defenders in the game. He logged seven tackles, one sack, one forced fumble, and two interceptions in a 2009 game against the Detroit Lions. Covering top wide receiver

Calvin Johnson, Woodson only gave up two catches and 10 yards. He was the NFC Defensive Player of the Week. Woodson ended the season with the Defensive Player of the Year award.

Woodson won the Super Bowl with the Packers in 2011. In his career, Woodson forced 33 fumbles, had 20 sacks, and logged 1,220 total tackles. He is tied for second in the NFL for interceptions returned for touchdowns with 11.

CHARLES WOODSON STATS

Fumbles Recovered	18
Touchdowns	13
Interceptions	65
Longest Interception Return	62 Yards

NO. 1 ROD WOODSON

Rod Woodson was the 10th overall pick in the 1987 NFL Draft. He started his career with the Pittsburgh Steelers and played there for 10 seasons. In his second season, he recorded 88 tackles and four interceptions.

Woodson played in the Pro Bowl each year from 1989 to 1994 and from 1999 to 2002. His 11 Pro Bowls are tied for fifth most in the NFL. Woodson is also a six-time First-Team

All-Pro. One of his best seasons was 1993 when he started all 16 games and recorded 95 tackles, two sacks, a touchdown, and eight interceptions. He won the NFL Defensive Player of the Year award that season.

In 1998, Woodson joined the Baltimore Ravens. Two seasons later, Woodson and the Ravens defeated the New York Giants in the Super Bowl. Woodson holds the NFL record for interceptions returned for a touchdown with 12. He is one of the best defensive players in NFL history.

ROD WOODSON STATS

Fumbles Recovered	32
Touchdowns	17
Interceptions	71
Longest Interception Return	98 Yards

EVEN MORE G.O.A.T.

There have been so many amazing cornerbacks in NFL history. Choosing only 10 is a challenge. Here are 10 others who could have made the G.O.A.T. list.

No. 11 ERIC ALLEN

No. 12 DWIGHT HICKS

No. 13 BOBBY BOYD

No. 14 DAVE BROWN

No. 15 ASANTE SAMUEL

No. 16 JOE LAVENDER

No. 17 GILL BYRD

No. 18 AENEAS WILLIAMS

No. 19 RONDE BARBER

No. 20 DARRELLE REVIS

YOUR G.O.A.T.

It's your turn to make a G.O.A.T. list about cornerbacks. Start by doing research. Consider the rankings in this book. Then check out the Learn More section on page 31. Explore the books and websites to learn more about football players of the past and present.

You can search online for more information about great players too. Check with a librarian, who may have other resources for you. You might even try reaching out to football teams or players to see what they think.

Once you're ready, make your list of the greatest players of all time. Then ask people you know to make G.O.A.T. lists and compare them. Do you have players no one else listed? Are you missing anybody your friends think is important? Talk it over and try to convince them that your list is the G.O.A.T.!

GLOSSARY

defense: the team trying to stop the other team from scoring

draft: when teams take turns choosing new players

end zone: the area at each end of a football field where players score touchdowns

First-Team All-Pro: a team made up of each season's best NFL players

fumble: when a football player loses hold of the ball while handling or running with it

interception: a pass caught by the defending team

Pro Bowl: the NFL's all-star game

return: when a player controls a kicked ball, interception, or fumble and carries it forward to gain yards

sack: when the quarterback is tackled for a loss of yards

tackle: to throw down or stop an opposing player with the ball in football

LEARN MORE

Football Team Facts for Kids
https://kids.kiddle.co/Football_team

Gilliam, Mickey. *Pro Football Upsets*. Minneapolis: Lerner Publications, 2020.

Holloway, Jerrett, and Thomas, Rafael. *Football: A Beginner's Guide: Learn the Basics to Watch and Enjoy the Game*. Oakland: Rockridge Press, 2022.

Levit, Joe. *Football's G.O.A.T.: Jim Brown, Tom Brady, and More*. Minneapolis: Lerner Publications, 2020.

Rod Woodson Pro Football Hall of Fame
https://www.profootballhof.com/players/rod-woodson/

What Does A Cornerback Do In Football?
https://www.rookieroad.com/football/questions/what-does-a-cornerback-do/

INDEX

PHOTO ACKNOWLEDGMENTS

Image credits:MediaNews Group/Bay Area News via Getty Images/Contributor/ Getty Images, p.4; MediaNews Group/Bay Area News via Getty Images/ Contributor/Getty Images, p.5; Michael Owens/Contributor/Getty Images, p.6; Eric Espada/Stringer/Getty Images, p.7; Kevin Casey/Stringer/Getty Images, p.8; Norm Hall/Contributor/Getty Images, p.9; Thearon W. Henderson/Contributor/Getty Images, p.10; Peter G. Aiken/Contributor/Getty Images, p.11; Focus On Sport/ Contributor/Getty Images, p.12; Focus On Sport/Contributor/Getty Images, p.13; Focus On Sport/Contributor/Getty Images, p.14; Focus On Sport/Contributor/ Getty Images, p.15; Clifton Boutelle/Contributor/Getty Images, p.16; Clifton Boutelle/Contributor/Getty Images, p.17; Bob Riha Jr/Contributor/Getty Images, p.18; Focus On Sport / Contributor/Getty Images, p.19; Bettmann/Contributor/ Getty Images, p.20; Bettmann/Contributor/Getty Images, p.21; Focus On Sport/ Contributor/Getty Images, p.22; HENNY RAY ABRAMS/Contributor/Getty Images, p.23; Joe Amon/Contributor/Getty Images, p.24; George Gojkovich/Contributor/ Getty Images, p.25; Owen C. Shaw/Contributor/Getty Images, p.26; Focus On Sport/Contributor/Getty Images, p.27

Cover: Allen Kee/Contributor/Getty Images; Tom Dahlin/Contributor/Getty Images; Focus On Sport/Contributor/Getty Images